ŞEHIT SEVDA SOCIETY

Abhijit Naskar is the twenty-first century Neuroscientist whose contributions in Cognitive and Behavioral Neuroscience have helped the world tackle the issues of systemic racism, prejudice, hate, extremism, discrimination and biases more effectively. As an untiring advocate of mental health and universal acceptance, he became a beloved best-selling author all over the world with his very first book "The Art of Neuroscience in Everything". With his pioneering ventures into the Neuropsychology of beliefs and biases, he has hugely contributed in the eradication of religious and cultural differences in our world, for which he is popularly hailed as the humanitarian scientist, who takes the human civilization in the path of sweet general harmony.

Şehit
Sevda
Society

Even in Death I Shall Live

ABHIJIT NASKAR

Also by Abhijit Naskar

The Art of Neuroscience in Everything
Your Own Neuron: A Tour of Your Psychic Brain
The God Parasite: Revelation of Neuroscience
The Spirituality Engine
Love Sutra: The Neuroscientific Manual of Love
Homo: A Brief History of Consciousness
Neurosutra: The Abhijit Naskar Collection
Autobiography of God: Biopsy of A Cognitive Reality
Biopsy of Religions: Neuroanalysis towards Universal
Tolerance
Prescription: Treating India's Soul
What is Mind?
In Search of Divinity: Journey to The Kingdom of Conscience
Love, God & Neurons: Memoir of a scientist who found
himself by getting lost
The Islamophobic Civilization: Voyage of Acceptance
Neurons of Jesus: Mind of A Teacher, Spouse & Thinker
Neurons, Oxygen & Nanak
The Education Decree
Principia Humanitas
The Krishna Cancer
Rowdy Buddha: The First Sapiens
We Are All Black: A Treatise on Racism
The Bengal Tigress: A Treatise on Gender Equality
Either Civilized or Phobic: A Treatise on Homosexuality
Wise Mating: A Treatise on Monogamy
Illusion of Religion: A Treatise on Religious
Fundamentalism
The Film Testament
Human Making is Our Mission: A Treatise on Parenting
I Am The Thread: My Mission
7 Billion Gods: Humans Above All
Lord is My Sheep: Gospel of Human
Morality Absolute
A Push in Perception
Let The Poor Be Your God
Conscience over Nonsense
Saint of The Sapiens
Time to Save Medicine
Fabric of Humanity
Build Bridges not Walls: In the name of Americana
The Constitution of The United Peoples of Earth

Lives to Serve Before I Sleep
When Humans Unite: Making A World Without Borders
All For Acceptance
Monk Meets World
Mission Reality
Citizens of Peace: Beyond The Savagery of Sovereignty
Operation Justice: To Make A Society That Needs No Law
See No Gender
The Gospel of Technology
Every Generation Needs Caretakers: The Gospel of
Patriotism
Aşkanjali: The Sufi Sermon
Mad About Humans: World Maker's Almanac
Revolution Indomable
When Call The People: My World My Responsibility
No Foreigner Only Family
Hurricane Humans: Give me accountability, I'll give you
peace
Ain't Enough to Look Human
Servitude is Sanctitude
Time To End Democracy: The Meritocratic Manifesto
I Vicdansaadet Speaking: No Rest Till The World is Lifted
Boldly Comes Justice: Sentient not Silent
Good Scientist: When Science and Service Combine
Sleepless for Society
Neden Türk: The Gospel of Secularism
Martyr Meets World: To Solve The Hard Problem of
Inhumanity
The Shape of A Human: Our America Their America
When Veins Ignite: Either Integration or Degradation
Heart Force One: Need No Gun to Defend Society
Solo Standing on Guard: Life Before Law
Generation Corazon: Nationalism is Terrorism
Mucize Insan: When The World is Family
Hometown Human: To Live for Soil and Society
Girl Over God: The Novel (Abi Naskar Adventures Book 1)
Gente Mente Adelante: Prejudice Conquered is World
Conquered
Earthquakin' Egalitarian: I Die Everyday So Your Children
Can Live
Giants in Jeans: 100 Sonnets of United Earth
Vatican Virus: The Forbidden Fiction (Abi Naskar
Adventures Book 2)

Karadeniz Chronicle: The Novel (Abi Naskar Adventures
Book 3)

DEDICATION

To The Citizens of Earth

CONTENTS

1. Endeavor, Explore and Expand.................................1

2. All of Us Are Shortsighted.........................5

3. Correction Over Criticism 9

4. For There to be Love on Earth 13

5. Wake Up From Death (The Sonnet)...................17

6. My Life is My Lesson to You 21

7. Be A Nut for The World...................25

8. Love in Exchange of Hate 29

9. What is Expansion 33

10. How Much Do You Need....................37

11. Call Me Nigga, But First 43

12. Actual Trinity...................47

13. Weakness Makes Us Human 51

14. Belief and Hate...................55

15. Bow, Bow and Bow Again...................59

16. Tu Lucha es Mi Lucha (El Soneto) 63

17. Your Struggle is My Struggle (The Sonnet).......67

18. Law of Sacrifice (The Sonnet) 71

19. Wipe Out The I (The Sonnet) 75

20. Your Culture is My Culture (The Sonnet)...........79

21. The One of My Heart (The Sonnet)...................83

22. Undestination (The Sonnet) 87

23. To Seduce You With Looks (The Sonnet).........91

24. To Live Amongst People 95

25. Forgive Us Jesus (The Sonnet)...................99

26.   Facts, Faith and Google 103

27.   We Are Not Our Ancestors.............................107

28.   Activism and Terrrorism................................111

29.   Be A Reformer, Not Deformer 115

30.   Raising Wholeness...119

31.   Either Defense or Peace................................123

32.   War Ain't Peace (The Sonnet)........................129

33.   Road to Sustainability 133

BIBLIOGRAPHY...139

1. Endeavor, Explore and Expand

Why do we live? Why do we die? How exactly are we supposed to make the journey from birth to death? Are we supposed to make it like every other newborn animal does, that is, driven by the basic evolutionary instinct of survival? Or are we supposed to do something different - are we supposed to achieve something different?

You ought to know by now, that we are not born to achieve some great dream - we are not born to do something different. If you haven't figured this out yet, then I'm afraid, there is no point in moving forward with our investigation.

We are born - period. What we do after we are born, that depends completely on us.

Do we spend life in the realization of a particular purpose? Do we stand ready to even die if necessary in the course of our purpose? And if we choose, not a life of purpose, but a life of primitive, chained existence instead, not unlike the animals, then are we at all living the life of a human?

I am not gonna answer that question. Because, my answer is irrelevant - what is relevant, is your own realization.

You've got to figure it yourself.

Figure out, what it is to be human.

Figure out, what it is to be not an animal.

Figure out, what it is to be civilized and not a savage.

Endeavor, explore and expand!

Upon your expansion lies assimilation - upon your expansion lies revolution - upon your expansion lies civilization.

But it ain't easy - not at all easy.

You know why?

Because your own biology is gonna keep you from expanding, at least most of your biology that is, for the capacity for growth lies dormant within your biology as well.

2. All of Us Are Shortsighted

Your biology doesn't want you to be inclusive - your biology doesn't want you to be global - your biology doesn't want you to be civilized - or to put it simply, your biology doesn't want you to be human - because to be human requires to be unselfish, which is deemed by your biology as a threat to your personal survival. Hence, it pulls all its savage strings in every walk of your life, so that you act as much selfish and primitive as possible, because as far as your biology is concerned, being selfish and primitive is what kept your ancestors alive in the jungle.

So, as far as your biology is concerned, why should things be any different for you now!

Your greatest enemy is your own biology - or neurobiology to be specific - a neurobiology that makes you selfish, a neurobiology that makes you racist, a neurobiology that makes you tribal, stereotypical and shortsighted.

All humans are shortsighted, because biases in your brain work 24/7 to keep you shortsighted.

If you want to be less shortsighted, you have to willingly and rather unpleasantly rebel against your biases, and for that you have to scrutinize every single one of your desires and beliefs, including the ones you hold most comforting.

And it all begins with a willful correction of yourself against a whole lot of objections from yourself.

Let me put it to you in simple terms. Civilization starts with self-correction. This one phrase - self-correction, holds the solution to all the troubles of our society and the world. It holds the solution to inequality - it holds the solution to discrimination - it holds the solution to prejudice and bigotry - it holds the solution to climate crisis – it holds the solution to every single human rights violation in the world.

3. Correction Over Criticism

But one thing I must mention - do not confuse correction with criticism. You do not need to criticize yourself, rather you need to realize your errors and take a firm but gentle stand to correct those errors. Once you can do that, your desire for self-correction would automatically inspire those around you, even if they are only few in numbers.

Change yourself and you shall inspire two more people in your neighborhood, from them four more, and from them eight more and so on. Thus, a movement of change sparked by one person will spread across the world like wildfire - slowly, but surely.

Let's start off with myself, so that you may find it less awkward to question yourself.

Let me tell you a secret if you haven't deduced it already. I hate violence - you know why, because I'm afraid - terribly afraid – every single minute of my existence - I'm afraid of myself - I'm afraid of my own rage - I'm afraid, that if I raise my hand at someone, there won't be any trace of them left.

When you raise your hand at someone, you have no idea, how many lives you are gonna destroy without even knowing it. So, raise your heart, not your hand.

Raise your heart, in conviction, in awareness, in character, and the world will have all the conviction, all the awareness, all the character it needs - in short, the world will have all the humanity it needs.

Humanity isn't going anywhere without your absolute and uncorrupted annihilation for the society. Let me simplify it. Without you, there is no progress - without you, there is no uplift - without you, there is no safety, sanity, security and serenity - without you, there is no humanity.

4. For There to be Love on Earth

Why stay silent, why stay asleep, why - why - why - no more - no more - wake up, wake up from indifference, wake up from practicality, wake up from mystical moronism - wake up and take charge - take charge with conscience, courage and compassion - throw all nonsense of magic, dogma and habit overboard, and stand up with a fresh breeze of reason and clarity in your heart. Only then - I repeat, only then shall the world know true progress - only then shall the world know true humanity.

No time for romance, no time for rigidity, no time for rituals - only sacrifice - that's what's needed - that's what the world demands, nay, that's what nature demands of you - for nature needs not you to sustain itself, but it does need you to discover the meaning of civilization, for anything civilized that can ever be born on this earth, it can only come from you, for all other animals are incapable of it, lacking the brain capacity to foster it in their skull.

It is true that even without us humans, there will still be life on earth, but let me tell you a greater truth - without us humans, there'll be no unconditional love in that life.

So for there to be life on earth, there is no need of humans, but for there to be love on earth, there must be humans. Or to be specific, for there to be love on earth, there must be you - there must be you standing strong with accountability coursing through your veins against the last trace of inhumanity.

I do not like using foul language, but sometimes foul language is the only language that can penetrate the thick skull of vegetables. So let me make an exception. Everybody fucks and leaves offspring, be the one to fight and leave a better society.

It is a selfish - selfish world - you know why - because nature teaches selfishness, parents teach selfishness, teachers teach selfishness - and by the time a child full of human potential grows up to be an adult, they are no longer human, they end up as modern savage in fancy rags.

5.   Wake Up From Death
(The Sonnet)

Wake Up From Death
(The Sonnet)

Wake up from death and return to life,
For as living dead we've been crawling for long.
Wake up from sanity and return to insanity,
For we've been insane in sanity for long.
Wake up from possibility, return to impossibility,
For we've been slave to the possible for long.
Wake up from reality and return to absurdity,
Habits of past have kept us hypnotized for long.
Wake up form truth and return to love,
For we've always confused assumptions with truth.
Wake up form ideology and return to the soil,
Integration means inclusion, not ideological coup.
Enough with nonchalance in the name of practicality!
Let us now rise as tornado and wipe out all apathy.

6.   My Life is My Lesson to You

Take the initiative my fiend - take the initiative to unlearn all those filthy teachings of primitivity, and be the first of a kind example of humanity for the world to draw lessons from.

How do you teach the world? You don't - you don't teach the world - you live your life as a lesson - then those who have the slightest desire for ascension of the self and the society, they reach out themselves to be your descendants. I have no desire to leave biological descendants, all I care about is to leave descendants who are related to me, not by blood, but by a common sense of responsibility towards the society.

In fact, I say it to you loud and clear. I'll be gone soon, but I'll leave behind enough soldiers to take care of this world for thousands of years.

Who are my soldiers - you - each and every one of you, who have recognized the God within themselves - the ones who rely not on a fictitious messiah, but stand up themselves as the living messiah against the massacres of magnanimity.

I may speak of hope when I'm speaking to others, but listen when I tell you, my soldier - I'm hopeless when it comes to you - I don't have any hope for you – 'cause my soldiers don't act on hope, they act on accountability.

So wake up, stand firm, and act, putting aside all romanticism. Why do you care for hope? Why do you care for belief? Why do you care for faith? The troubles of society are far too big to be solved by those phony words. They need actual, tangible, steady hands – hands that don't abhor dirt - hands that ain't scared to bleed.

7.   Be A Nut for The World

Death itself should be afraid of you - such oughta be your resolve - resolve of a soldier - resolve of a human - no humanitarian, no activist, no nothing - just human.

No name, no background, no ancestry, nothing - you identity is your purpose - your identity is your work - your identity is your accountability - your identity is your sacrifice.

You are my şehit sevda society - you are my martyr love society - you are no cult, you are no religion, you are free - free as a bird - yet not a bird, for you are a human, who flies out of accountability, not recklessness. Birds fly to take care of their family, whereas you fly to take care of not just your family, but all the families in your neighborhood.

One person caring for one neighborhood, that's how we'll change the world, not with policy and policing.

But mark you, caring for a neighborhood doesn't mean to walk around like pompous nimrods calling the cops on black folks. Caring for a neighborhood means standing firm against discrimination, bigotry and suffering for all the past, present and future residents of that neighborhood, as well as for the visitors and travelers.

And again, don't aim for some phony idealistic perfection. All I'm asking of you is that - if you want to see yourself as human, then act as human - not as a tribal nut, not as a religious nut, not as an intellectual nut - but as a human nut. If you must be a nut, be a nut for humanity, be a nut for the humans, be a nut for the world.

You see, lasting planetary peace cannot be attained by chasing after petty nationalistic insecurities. For that we must be whole, whole human beings. Individual wholeness brings individual nonsectarianism, and individual nonsectarianism brings global unification.

8. Love in Exchange of Hate

Unification is not a concept of some pompous philosophy. Unification is just a by-product of love. Or to put it another way, unification is just a simple outcome of love. They keep bickering over whether there is life after death. I say, to hell with life after death, ask instead, is there life after love!

And the answer is, no, there isn't, for love is life, and hate is death.

Once a man came up to me on the street and asked furiously, 'you keep shouting about religious harmony - what is your own religion?' I smiled and said, 'if you are catholic, think of me as a muslim and hit me - if you are a muslim, think of me as a kafir and hit me - if you are an atheist, think of me as a believer and hit me - because my friend, to love in exchange of hate, is my religion.'

The man lowered his head and without saying a word, walked away.

However, I despise talking in riddles. So let me make it absolutely clear. To love in exchange of hate, doesn't mean letting them hurt your loved ones while you stand silent and watch them being hurt.

The point is, you must restrain the oppressor without causing harm yourself.

So for example, if someone tries to harm you or your loved ones, restrain them, but do not hit them back. Think of them as your own children. If your child attacks you with a knife, would you snatch the knife from their hands and strike them back. No, you simply take the knife away from them, so that they don't do any harm to anybody.

I ain't askin' you to be better - I am askin' you to be civilized. Nonviolence is the foundation of civilization, but first we must ask, what is nonviolence?

No matter what my good friend Jesus said two thousand years ago, nonviolence doesn't mean nonresistance to evil, nonviolence means restraining evil without retaliating with further evil.

Peace begins with love and love begins when we get rid of our vengeful spirit, and foster a sense of responsibility in its place. It is this sense of responsibility that turns an animal into a human.

9. What is Expansion

What are you? Where is your responsibility? I'm not criticizing. I'm not judging. I'm simply asking, so that you may ask yourself - without judgment, without assumption, without prejudice - just out of sheer curiosity, for when you learn to question yourself out of sheer curiosity, that's when from the depth of your mind rises clarity.

Clarity comes from curiosity, and curiosity comes from a desire for expansion. If you are willing to expand, the world will expand. But if you refute all expansion and cling to the tenets of tradition because it's comforting, then I'm afraid, that very illusory comfort will turn into your and the world's darkest nightmare.

Love your tradition, sure, but not at the cost of expansion. Mark you, I say expansion, not advancement. Because to the materialistic morons of the world advancement is code for destruction, mechanization and exploitation.

I am not talking about such advancement. We need advancement that not only raises external conditions of life, but also internal ones, and that too, for everybody, not just the elites.

Exploitation is not expansion, mechanization is not expansion, destruction of nature is not expansion. Let me tell you what expansion means.

Expansion means assimilation - expansion means collectivism - expansion means a healthy balance between the green of nature and green of dollar - expansion means mechanization with the purpose of the alleviation of suffering, not the alleviation of activity.

10. How Much Do You Need

Life lies in expansion, not in luxury. In fact, luxury is as crippling a force as abject poverty. One of the primary reasons of disparities is our inability to distinguish between necessity and luxury. Let me demonstrate, and for that, let me ask you a simple question.

How many t-shirts and pairs of pants do you own?

Think.

Once you have a basic idea of the quantity, then ask yourself, do you actually need so many t-shirts and pants - and I mean need, not want!

Now let me tell you how many t-shirts I own.

Three – yes, three.

I have three t-shirts and three pairs of jeans. And I'll use them as casual wear for at least a year before I discard them. Other than them I have two blue shirts and two blazers for public appearances. That's about all. One of the shirts is the one you see me wearing in my book covers.

Upon fulfilling your actual necessity, use your excess resources to lift the society however you see fit. But do it at the grassroots, instead of going big.

What I mean is that, if you have a couple hundred dollars which you'd like to use to lift the society, instead of donating it to some big and famous charity organization, use it to help the local businesses or communities in your locality or your city.

This way you'd not only reduce the abuse of your resources a great deal, but more importantly, you are actually being involved in the uplift of people quite directly. You see, it's not about you callously giving away your resources, it's about you consciously using your resources for the elevation of the fallen.

And the same holds true for reparations. Financial reparations may ease economic disparity to some extent, but it doesn't end psychological disparity. Let me demonstrate.

Let's assume you are the conscientious descendant of a slave owner. And driven by your conscience you track down the descendants of the slaves owned by your ancestor and give them back every penny that your ancestor owes their ancestors.

This may provide them with a financial aid, but still it won't end the racial discrimination they'll continue to face in society - the discrimination that all of us non-white folks face in the so-called civilized parts of the world.

11. Call Me Nigga, But First

Civilization that hasn't learnt to move past color, is no civilization. It is a mere mockery of civilization. I am not talking about all that nonsense of not seeing color. The problem is not that you see color, the problem is that you assume character from color.

Come close, be my buddy, then after a while call me nigga - it won't affect our friendship one bit. But out of the blue if you walk up to me as a complete stranger and call me that, then you only deepen the wounds caused by white oppressors throughout human history.

The context makes all the difference. Think of sibling rivalry for example. Isn't there name-calling amongst siblings, and rather ugly ones at that! But does that affect their bond with each other! It doesn't. Because they know in their heart that at the end of the day, they are there for each other.

Likewise, lay your life for others no matter their color and culture, and they'll walk to the ends of the earth for you. Call it service, call it social work, call it activism, call it humanitarianism, call it whatever you like. But I call it plain humanity.

What is humanity - humans thinking of humans, that's humanity.

It is that simple - no ideology needed - no philosophy needed - no intellect needed - all that is needed is an uncorrupted accountability! Remember, liberty doesn't make a society civilized, accountability does.

Unrestrained liberty eventually leads to recklessness and cruelty, hence inhumanity. But if there is accountability, it automatically ensures liberty for each and every member of society. And by accountability I'm not talking about a cold mechanical sense of logicality, rather what I'm talking about is a warm and ever-growing sense of responsibility.

12. Actual Trinity

Civilization requires three things - warmth, reason and courage - all of which come to life on their own when there is accountability.

These three are the real trinity of a civilized society. And each responsible individual is the source and vessel of this trinity. Or to put it another way, each responsible individual is the walking trinity of civilization - the only trinity of the world. We are the Father, the Son and the Holy Ghost - that's about it.

There's no mystery to it. There's no magic to it. And most definitely, there's no bible involved in it. I have nothing against the bible. It is just a book, like any other book. And like any other book, it is not flawless - or to be more accurate, it is not the universal measure of rightful living for beings of all ages.

But this doesn't mean that I am an advocate for pure and absolute logic or reason. I am not. I'll say it to you plainly. I'm not gonna check whether you go to church or not, I'm not gonna check whether you read the bible or not, I'm not gonna check whether you have a subscription of the Scientific American or not - all I care about is, whether you help a stranger or not.

I don't want an atheist world, I just want a human world. Because just like there are religious nuts tearing this world apart in the name of faith, there are also atheist nuts, who are doing the same except in the name of reason and facts. And I stand firm against both with the last drop of blood in my veins, in order to defend the rights of all humans, and strengthen the course of integration.

Integration happens neither through bible-babble nor through reason-treason. What is reason-treason you ask! Reason used to lift society is reason, but reason used to belittle others is treason, for it is an abuse of reason – hence, an inhuman use of reason.

Integration happens by acknowledging people's weakness and lifting them up, while standing by them as long as it takes, instead of mocking them for their weakness.

13. Weakness Makes Us Human

But again like always, things are not as simple as they appear. Remember, there's a difference between weakness and inhumanity. So, you must foster the capacity to distinguish between harmless weakness and harmful meanness.

Let me give you an example. Many people need their faith in order to survive. It may be considered a weakness in some respect, but it is a weakness that you must learn to accept without judgment, for we all have weaknesses similar to this. And these very weaknesses make us human.

That weakness turns into meanness or sheer inhumanity when the harmless sense of faith is replaced with a sense of supremacy over all other faiths. The same holds true, when our sense of intellect turns into a sense of intellectual supremacy. It has nothing to do with reason or belief, and everything to do with how we behave with others.

This is why, unless I'm on stage to actually give a talk, I don't like to talk wise when I'm in public. Humility is not my weakness, it is what keeps me awake to life, for there is nothing more blinding than arrogance.

When your shadow grows bigger than you, know that your downfall is near. And indeed, after a brief flight of progress, the downfall of not just the individual humans, but the whole of humankind is now near!

You know why! Because before it was ignorance that used to destroy society, now in its place has arrived fancy, pompous, intellectual arrogance - arrogance in front of which human frailty is unacceptable - in front of which anything that is not logical is revolting.

To be honest, it's not really that different from the old days. It's just a new kind of ignorance, an ignorance of humility, an ignorance of acceptability, an ignorance of simplicity - or to put it simply, an ignorance of humanity.

14. Belief and Hate

I'll say it to you plainly. Facts don't make us human, faith doesn't make us human, what makes us human is our willingness to step across facts and faith to lend a hand of humanity.

Be a hand - not a christian hand, jewish hand, muslim hand, or atheist hand - just a hand - not a black hand, white hand, brown hand or yellow hand - just a hand - not a straight hand or queer hand - just a hand - a hand that helps and a hand that heals.

No intellect is higher than humanity, just like no faith is higher than humanity. If your faith empowers and expands your humanity, then more power to it I say! If your intellect empowers and expands your humanity, then more power to it! But if any of them becomes a hindrance to your humanity, you must throw them away as far as possible.

For example, I don't need God, you may not need God, but you have no right to belittle someone who needs the comfort of their deity in order to survive, as long as they are not practicing hate and bigotry. Let me give you another example to put it into perspective.

I have no affinity towards sports, but I hold no grudge against those who do. If a few hours of sports make their life a bit less stressful, what's wrong with that! This holds true for sports, God and a million other things, for a person can't live on logic alone.

Any belief that doesn't make you hateful is a good belief. It is this simple. It doesn't have to be logical, it doesn't have to be based on facts. It doesn't even have to make the slightest sense. It just has to be nonconducive to hate and segregation.

15. Bow, Bow and Bow Again

Life is no life if there are no people in it. And if you let your intellect or faith take over your psyche, then slowly but surely all trace of humanity will eventually disappear from your behavior, and you'll end up as either a filthy savage driven by prejudice or a cold, heartless computer driven by facts.

Let me put it to you in simple terms. The lower you bow in front of the helpless, the higher you rise in front of the world. Reach out my friend - reach out to someone who has no one, and tell them - ben buradayım, her zaman burada olacağım - I'm here, I'll always be here. Tell them, tu lucha es mi lucha – your struggle is my struggle.

If you haven't been there for someone other than yourself, then what is the point of you my friend! What is the point of any of us, if we can't step up to take it upon ourselves to remove the clouds of suffering from the lives forgotten by the suited savages of this world!

Have a tremendous drive to give yourself up for the benefit of others, no matter whether you get anything in return. Everybody loves to be loved, there's nothing special about it. Such love is no different form animal love. Be human. How you ask! Be a one-sided lover to the whole humanity.

Be the incorruptible comet of conscience and compassion, that cleanse this cockeyed world of all its cockiness. Be humble, don't tremble, when the people call, with your life do the gamble. Remember, when you love, you are immortal, when you hate, you are already dead, despite being alive.

Savor the sacrifice, for in sacrifice lies the happiness that we seek our whole life - sacrifice for a purpose, sacrifice for a people, sacrifice for a world. That's all there is to it really - to the elevation of not just the society, but of your own life as well.

16. Tu Lucha es Mi Lucha
(El Soneto)

Tu Lucha es Mi Lucha
(El Soneto)

Tu lucha es mi lucha,
Porque mi paraíso está en tu sonrisa.
Tu problema es mi problema,
Porque mi victoria está en tu alegría.
Sin ti, mi vida no es vida,
Porque la vida sin amor es muerte.
Sin ti, mis logros no son logros,
Sin ti, pierdo el coraje.
Solo tú eres la luz de mis ojos,
Sin ti soy un barco sin brújula.
Eres la fuerza de mis venas,
Sin ti, me convierto en gelatina.
Mi cielo y mi tierra eres tú.
El aliento de mi vida eres tú.

17. Your Struggle is My Struggle
(The Sonnet)

Your Struggle is My Struggle
(The Sonnet)

Your struggle is my struggle,
'Cause my heaven is in your smile.
Your trouble is my trouble,
Without you by my side all victory is vile.
My life is only life when you are in it,
For a life without love is but death in disguise.
Without you my achievements mean nothing,
'Cause you're the sweetness of all my flight.
You are the light of my eyes,
Without you I am but a ship without compass.
You are the strength coursing through my veins,
Without you I turn into worthless abscess.
You are my sky, my land and my ocean.
The breath of my life is you and my salvation.

18. Law of Sacrifice
(The Sonnet)

Law of Sacrifice
(The Sonnet)

The more you give life,
The more you'll have life.
The more you give light,
The more you'll have light.
The more the I gets lost in others,
The more you'll end all bigoted strife.
The more you take pain for those around,
The more you'll know the joy of life.
Worst of all superstitions is selfishness,
It keeps an animal from becoming human.
Let the mind be cleansed of all self,
So our heart becomes a mirror for every person.
Reject all selfishness that makes you cold and blind.
Sacrifice is the law behind all love and light.

75   **19. Wipe Out The I
                        (The Sonnet)**

Wipe Out The I
(The Sonnet)

Once a person gives up all for others,
They'll achieve everything worth achieving.
The art of self-discovery is in self-annihilation,
Whereas self-obsession only causes suffering.
Once a person is insane with the sacrificial spirit,
They'll know the meaning of civilized sanity.
Once a person feels the joy of selflessness,
All worldly pleasures will turn into foul vanity.
Once a person hones the power of simplicity,
They'll trash all trace of pomposity from life.
Once a person senses the valor of humility,
They'll discard all arrogant divide.
Life is simple, but we mess it up with selfishness.
Wipe out the I, and you will taste its sweetness.

20. Your Culture is My Culture
(The Sonnet)

Your Culture is My Culture
(The Sonnet)

With infinite love brimming in my heart,
I have arrived at your doorstep.
Please, I beg you, do not turn me back,
Let me in, so I may be one with your footstep.
It's not my fault, I wasn't born in your culture,
Yet I've assimilated your culture as my own.
Please do not throw me out my dear friend,
Standing together our powers will be honed.
I may not speak your native tongue,
I may not be familiar with your way of life.
But do you not smile like me when in joy,
Like me do you not shed tears when in strife!
Here I stand at your door with my arms stretched.
Hold it with affection or chop it off if you so elect.

21. The One of My Heart
(The Sonnet)

The One of My Heart
(The Sonnet)

I see the one of my heart,
In every direction, in every face.
Yet I won't say a word,
In silence I'll bear all coldness.
You may throw me out of your heart,
But you can't oust yourself from mine.
You are in every pore of my being,
You are my only lifeline.
You are the one that runs in my nerves,
As the power-grid of my mind.
The pain of being a one-sided lover,
Is sweeter to me than a thousand goldmines.
Cuss me, mock me, hurt me all you like.
All I care about is to be an aid in your life.

22. Undestination
(The Sonnet)

Undestination

(The Sonnet)

I gave up my country in your love,
I gave up my home for your sweetness.
I stand at your door without identity,
Will you take me in and fill my emptiness!
I've sailed my ship towards undestination,
Let the waves take me where they may.
Embracing the unknown I became a pal of all.
Come out my friend from your cage of dismay.
Come with me, and we'll explore all impossibility.
If we must be awful let's be awful together.
Let us lose all maps and walk around as vagrants.
Why worry, when we have each other!
To hell with destination, let us savor the journey!
Before success and achievement, let us first have unity.

23. To Seduce You With Looks
(The Sonnet)

To Seduce You With Looks
(The Sonnet)

I haven't come to seduce you with looks,
I have come to overwhelm you with love.
I haven't come to break your door by force,
I've come to charm it open with my mind's touch.
I haven't come to bring you worldly riches,
But to offer you the garland of my heart.
I haven't come to usher you with complements,
I've come to celebrate you, tearing myself apart.
I haven't come to count the benefits of bond,
I've come to make you lose count of your wounds.
I haven't come to feel butterflies in my stomach,
But to fight the world, helping you break all rules.
Let me burn to ashes time and time again,
So I may remove the shadows from your life's lane.

24. To Live Amongst People

Lay yourself down for others, and you'll fly higher than you can imagine. This may appear to be base to some, but pay no attention to their ramblings whatsoever.

I'm mentioning the term base, particularly because, it's a term that's often used by my haters.

And you know why they call me base - because I don't shout about the supremacy of intellect and logic all the time. That is why many even call me a religious nut - because, I stand firm at the frontline of religious harmony against the inhuman advances of intellectual bigots as well as religious bigots.

I am the wind, I just want to flow amongst the people without any barrier. I have no desire to prove the supremacy of facts where there's no need. Some days you may find me in the church taking part in the choir and singing out loud praising my humanitarian predecessor most enthusiastically. Other days, you may find me talking shop with a bunch of atheist scientists. I am in everybody, everybody is in me.

Also here one thing I must mention. Just like there are atheist scientists, there are also theist scientists. For example, one of the pillars of modern neurology is V. S. Ramachandran, who often dedicates his works to Saraswati, the Hindu goddess of wisdom. You know why? Because even we scientists need our imaginary friends. My imaginary friend is my late teacher G.C., and I often find it comforting to talk to him as if he's listening.

And upon listening to all this, if you still cannot figure out what I myself believe in, in terms of religion, then I'm afraid you're wasting your time reading me. All my beliefs, all my ideas, all my dreams revolve around one thing and one thing alone - the uplift of people. And you are not gonna lift the people by calling them religious nuts, just because they don't happen to be nonbelievers.

25. Forgive Us Jesus
(The Sonnet)

Forgive Us Jesus
(The Sonnet)

Forgive us Jesus, my friend,
We couldn't walk in your footsteps.
You asked us to love our neighbor,
Yet we found it impossible to be hateless.
You didn't hate those who hated you,
You loved them despite being mocked.
Yet we can't even talk without judging today,
We can't accept any difference in thought.
Forgetting all comfort and luxury,
You gave your life trying to erase bigotry.
Yet we made you fodder for our own prejudice,
And turned the crucifix into a badge of cruelty.
We used you my friend to deepen our division.
We prefer mindless worship over hearty compassion.

26. Facts, Faith and Google

It is true that even I use the term religious nuts, but never have I used them or will ever use them to refer to everybody who believes in a supernatural entity or force. I use the term exclusively to refer to those who raise barriers in society in the name of faith, just like I use the term intellectual nuts to refer to those who raise barriers in society in the name of facts, in the name of intellectualism.

As far as I'm concerned, facts that don't elevate the human condition are nothing but fiction. Facts and faith all come later, beyond your bloody intellect, first be a humanizer.

I've spent my life in the study of facts, and I'm very much aware of their great power. But from five minutes of googling if you think, just because facts have power they are gonna do good to society, then you couldn't be more wrong. Whether power does good or not, depends on the person using that power.

Let's conduct a thought experiment shall we! Let's assume you find out a fact that I'm not aware of, and come up to me to tell me all about it along with all the evidence to back it up! And I'll accept it most enthusiastically. But then what! What are you going to do with that particular fact? How are you going to use that fact to elevate the people around you - to elevate your society - to elevate the world?

And that's where science differs from atheism. Atheism thrives on facts, whereas science is not simply about discovering facts, science is about discovering facts and then applying them for the betterment of society.

27. We Are Not Our Ancestors

Forget how our ancestors lived their lives. We no longer can pledge our allegiance to either faith or facts. It is time we step across both - it is time we become the pedestrians of humanity, rather than wasting our life as pedestrians of narrowness - be it the narrowness of faith or facts.

Anything that impedes your humanity is nothing but a chain. Till now it was faith and tradition that have been the prime impediment in our course of humanity, now a new enemy has risen - it's called absolute, unquestionable logicality.

So shred all chains to dust my friend, and advance as actual liberated beings, liberated not just from the primitive hogwash of magic and mysticism, but also from the modern hogwash of intellectual condescension. Advance my soldier, advance as a whole human being, accepting the good from every walk of society.

For example, I am no socialist, I am no capitalist - I am a whole human being, and I accept the good wherever I find it, that could potentially benefit society. As I've said countless times, we must step across all duality, particularly the dualities in ideology and philosophy.

There ought to be one supreme ideology - one supreme philosophy - one supreme purpose, ahead of all else - the uplift of people - the uplift of society - the uplift of the world. But again, stepping across dualities doesn't mean turning blind to the limitations of the world and the reality we live in.

Think of the infinity, feel the infinity, be the infinity, but then come back to the finite and apply your realization for the betterment of your current reality. You are to be nondualistic, not so you could mock at the world, but so you could lift the world.

But mark you, lifting the world has nothing to do with activism, because it is one of the most shallow words of our time. Let's figure out why.

28. Activism and Terrrorism

There's not one, but two kinds of activism. One is responsible activism and another is reckless activism. And it is responsible activism that leads to the reform of society, whereas reckless activism causes nothing but harm in the name of change.

Let me give you an example. As I just saw yesterday on my twitter feed, a bunch of eco-terrorists, who call themselves climate-activist blocked traffic in London leading to quite a ruckus. But I am not against the protest part. What got me ticked off is when they didn't even let pass an ambulance carrying an elderly patient headed for the hospital to receive cancer treatment.

First law of responsible activism - make way for the ambulance, otherwise, there's no difference between you and a petty terrorist. To these people I say, get your priorities straight first - do you want to tackle climate crisis or do more harm deluded by the fallacy that you are doing good by causing disorder.

The line between activism and terrorism is so thin that if you scratch the surface of all the activists, you'll end up discovering more terrorists than actual reformers. And this is why, I've grown an utter disgust for the term activist.

And one more thing I say to the climate activists. If you actually want to tackle climate crisis, then instead of yelling at the politicians like a hysterical Karen and obstructing traffic, educate the masses on clean energy and get involved in startups working on affordable clean energy solutions.

29. Be A Reformer, Not Deformer

Let me give it to you straight, fossil fuel still rules the world not because the fossil fuel industry is all-powerful, but because clean energy solution is still not convenient and affordable enough for everyday home use.

Yes, there are many startups who are working to solve this particular problem, and they are the ones who'll ultimately solve the problem of carbon emission, not the moronic ramblings of those eco-nutjobs.

Here some may argue, am I not a nutjob as well! To which I say – yes, I'm a nutjob as well, but I know when to tighten my nuts and when to let them hang loose - pun absolutely intended!

The point is, be a reformer, not a deformer. Remember, the moment a cause starts causing harm instead of good, it's no longer a cause, but a farce. And that's where the need arises for the evolution of the term revolution. Harm on even a single human life can't be considered a collateral damage, like it used to be in the past.

We don't just need revolution, we need civilized revolution. So before you go about rebelling against the norms of the society, first have a clear grasp of what revolution ought to mean in a civilized world. It's no longer about picking up arms and going into the battlefield to slaughter the enemy.

I say it to you in plain words - not a single life should be harmed - restrain them if they commit a harm in front of your eyes, but do not, I repeat, do not harm them. Sometimes it's gonna be difficult, extremely difficult, but despite all urge to retaliate harm with more harm, restrain yourself from doing so, 'cause only then, we shall be able to build a paradigm of actual lasting peace.

Make no mistake - I am not asking you to stay silent, I am asking, nay, time demands of you to stand up, but without doing harm. Remember, revolution means re-evolution, that is, constant evolution - it doesn't mean de-evolution, that is, backward evolution.

30. Raising Wholeness

We humans are sucker for soft power. Be strong of nerves but soft of heart, and you'll make a deeper and more lasting impact upon the fabric of society than all the toughness in the world. More people will start walking in your footsteps inspired by your sacrificial spirit than if you beg them to join you.

If you wanna leave a heritage for your offspring, leave behind the heritage of sacrifice, leave behind the heritage of bravery, leave behind the heritage of compassionate reasoning. Make not the mistake like our ancestors did, to leave behind the heritage of mindless rituals and baseless beliefs.

If you wanna pass on a ritual to your children, pass on the ritual of helping - if you wanna pass on a belief to your children, pass on the belief, to never discriminate others based on belief. Bigots may call this 'activating the children', but I call this - raising human beings.

We still live in a tribal world, because our ancestors were tribal and they raised their children as such. No more I say. Raise human beings, not tribal fiends. Be whole yourself, raise your children as whole, and soon the entire world will be whole.

Policy is an artificial way to change the world. Change in policy without a change in the mindset of the citizens, in time brings civil war down on a nation. You see, the bigots and supremacists do not simply disappear because some progressive politician bans inhuman behavior.

Mark you, I'm not saying that progressive policies are a bad thing. What I'm pointing out is that, if you think once you change a policy, that's it, you'd achieve all the change you could ever dream of, then you couldn't be more wrong.

31. Either Defense or Peace

Change in the mindset of a nation's citizens starts at home. And the reformers of a home are parents and teachers. If you wanna transform a nation's future, first and foremost, elevate the conditions of parents and teachers.

Mark my words, cut your defense budget to the bare minimum and siphon those funds to initiatives empowering parents and teachers, and within fifty years your nation will become a super-power on the face of earth. And in the process you'll not only reduce societal disparities in your nation drastically, but also your national crime rate will plummet like crazy.

Yet you won't - that is, the politicians won't, out of sheer primeval insecurity, just like those anti-vaxxers who wouldn't inoculate their children out of sheer primeval insecurity. And this way, if the anti-vaxxers are conspiracy nuts, which they sure are, so are the politicians, who keep dumping billions and billions of dollars in defense contracts out of sheer primitive insecurity instead of working to organize peace.

In case of our US, the figure is in hundreds – over seven hundred billion to be specific, for the Fiscal Year 2021.

How come those suited savages can't fathom this simple fact that, you can't organize peace by expanding your military, you organize peace by empowering your citizens. With the lollypop of nationalism they've even seduced the complacent citizens to believe that having a large military is a matter of pride.

When a nation's defense budget overwhelms its spending on education, know that something is fundamentally wrong with that nation. Yet this very wrong is accepted as the most rightful norm in this so-called modern society.

So when I speak of slashing defense funds, all the politicians, most at least, will jump down my throat with the excuse that they can't just cut down the defense budget on a whim - there are implications!

To which I say, I'm more aware of those implications as a behaviorist than you are as a representative.

But for the sake of the discourse, let's assume that you can't indeed cut down the defense budget. Now my response is this.

Many politicians skim from the government's spending anyway, all I ask is that you skim some more from the defense budget, officially of course, and siphon it to priority sectors like education, healthcare and housing.

**32. War Ain't Peace
(The Sonnet)**

War Ain't Peace
(The Sonnet)

Hudson, Thames, Nile and Sindhu,
All are now red with the blood of the innocent.
Who is to blame for such catastrophe,
Everybody who accepts arms race as upliftment.
Suited savages have seduced them to believe,
That bigger the military greater the pride.
It's necessary for politicians to sell nationalism,
Or else their loyal subjects will all get untied.
Acts of national security only breed insecurity,
Which forces people to seek comfort in weapons.
True, lasting stability and serenity of a nation,
Comes only from a universal desire for union.
Let the politicians sell war in the name of peace.
Why must the citizens buy it like rats chasing cheese!

33. Road to Sustainability

However, I accept that defense is necessary, but it is high time that little by little you start shifting your attention from defense to endeavors with actual potential for building a stable nation and a stable world, unless of course, the very word peace is absent from your dictionary.

And this stability has nothing to do with the military capacities of a nation, nor has it anything to do with economic growth. This stability that I'm talking about, has another fancy name, which may be more appealing to people. And that term is sustainability.

But there is a problem with the term sustainability. You see, politicians around the world have convinced their citizens that sustainability means economic growth. And that's where all the trouble begins.

The world doesn't need economic growth, it needs sustainability, and sustainability and economic growth are not the same thing. Let's investigate why.

In the world we live in economic growth doesn't actually mean collective economic growth, it is actually code for selective economic growth, which means, exclusive prosperity of a select group of people.

You see, economic growth founded on selfishness doesn't bring sustainability, it only causes more economic disparity. And whether that disparity appears to be progress or not to you, depends on which side of the disparity you belong to.

So I say again, stop obsessing over economic growth, start thinking of sustainability - collective sustainability. All the selfishness in the world won't bring us sustainability, what will is a common interest for collective growth in all of us. And that all begins with the I. It starts with you.

So do whatever is in your power to bring sustainability in your neighborhood, leave the rest to nature. Be a responsible neighbor, and the world will have all the responsible citizens it needs. Whatever is selfish, is unsustainable, whatever is unselfish, is sustainable.

But again, what you must keep in mind is that, I'm talking about civilized sustainability, because the jungle is sustainable in its own way, and if that's the kind of sustainability we really want, then there was no need for us to sever ties with nature in the first place, we could've continued to live in the jungle along with our fellow animals, like animals.

So, it comes down to one simple question - what kind of sustainability do you really want, sustainability fraught with serenity or sustainability fraught with cruelty? Don't go about seeking the answer here and there, for the answer you seek, is you yourself.

BIBLIOGRAPHY

Archer M., (2000), Being Human: The Problem of Agency. Cambridge University Press.

Adolphs R (2003) Cognitive neuroscience of human social behaviour. Nature Rev Neurosci 4: 165–178.

Adolphs R, Tranel D, Damasio AR (2003) Dissociable neural systems for recognizing emotions. Brain Cogn 52: 61–69.

Andresen, Jensine, and Robert Forman, eds. Cognitive Models and Spiritual Maps. Bowling Green, Ohio: Imprint Academic, 2000.

Azari, Nina, Janpeter Nickel, Gilbert Wunderlich, Michael Niedeggen, Harald Hefter, Lutz Tellmann, Hans Herzog, Petra Stoerig, Dieter Birnbacher, and Rudiger Seitz. "Neural Correlates of Religious Experience."

European Journal of Neuroscience 13, no. 8 (2001)

Agar, N. (2004). Liberal eugenics: In defence of human enhancement. London: Blackwell Publishing.

Alteheld, N., Roessler, G., Vobig, M., & Walter, R. (2004). The retina implant new approach to a visual prosthesis. Biomedizinische Technik, 49(4), 99–103.

Antal, A., Nitsche, M. A., Kincses, T. Z., Kruse, W., Hoffmann, K. P., & Paulus, W. (2004a). Facilitation of visuo-motor learning by transcranial direct current stimulation of the motor and extrastriate visual areas in humans. European Journal of Neuroscience, 19(10), 2888–2892.

Bernstein R.J., (1971), Praxis and Action: Contemporary Philosophies of Human Activity. Philadelphia: University of Pennsylvania Press.

Bernstein R.J., (1976), The Restructuring Social and Political Thought.

Bernstein R.J., (1983), Beyond Relativism and Objectivism: Science, Hermeneutics, and Praxis. Philadelphia: University of Pennsylvania Press.

Bernstein R.J., (1986), Philosophical Profiles. Philadelphia: University of Pennsylvania Press.

Bernstein R.J., (1991), New Constellation. Cambridge: MIT Press.

Birkhead, T. R., Johnson, S. D. & Nettleship, D. N. (1985). Extra-pair matings and mate guarding in the common murre Uria aalge. - Anim. Behav. 33, p. 608-619.

Beauregard, Mario, and Vincent Paquette. "Neural Correlates of a Mystical Experience in Carmelite Nuns." Neuroscience Letters 405, no. 3 (2006)

Benson, Herbert. Timeless Healing: The Power and Biology of Belief. New York: Scribner, 1996

Bose, Subhas Chandra. An Indian Pilgrim: An Unfinished Autobiography, Oxford University Press, 1997

Bogen, J.E.(1995a), 'On the neurophysiology of consciousness: Part I. An overview', Consciousness and Cognition, 4.

Bogen, J.E. (1995b), 'On the neurophysiology of consciousness: Part II. Constraining the semantic problem', Consciousness and Cognition, 4.

Bremner, J. D., R. Soufer, et al. (2001). "Gender differences in cognitive and neural correlates of remembrance of emotional words." Psychopharmacol Bull 35 (3).

Brothers, L. (2002). The social brain: A project for integrating primate behavior and neurophysiology in a new domain. In J. T. Cacioppo et al. (Eds.), Foundations in neuroscience. Cambridge, MA: MIT Press.

Buss, D. D. (2003). Evolutionary Psychology: The New Science of Mind, 2nd ed. New York: Allyn & Bacon.

Buss, D. M. (1989). "Conflict between the sexes: Strategic interference and the evocation of anger and upset." J Pers Soc Psychol 56 (5).

Buss, D. M. (1995). "Psychological sex differences. Origins through sexual selection." Am Psychol 50 (3).

Buss, D. M., and D. P. Schmitt (1993). "Sexual strategies theory: An evolutionary perspective on human mating." Psychol Rev 100 (2).

Blakemore SJ, Decety J (2001) From the perception of action to the understanding of intention. Nature Rev Neurosci 2: 561.

Colapietro V., (1988), "Human Agency: The Habits of Our Being." Southern Journal of Philosophy, XXVI, 2, pp. 153-68.

Colapietro V., (1992), "Purpose, Power, and Agency." The Monist, 75, 4 (October) pp. 423-44.

Colapietro V., (2004a), "C. S. Peirce's Reclamation of Teleology." Nature in American Philosophy, ed. Jean De Groot (Washington, D.C.: Catholic University Press of America), pp. 88-108.

Carey DP, Perrett DI, Oram MW (1997) Recognizing, understanding and reproducing actions. In: Jeannerod M, Grafman J (eds) Handbook of neuropsychology. Vol. 11: Action and cognition. Elsevier, Amsterdam.

Carr L, Iacoboni M, Dubeau MC, Mazziotta JC, Lenzi GL (2003) Neural mechanisms of empathy in humans: a relay from neural systems for imitation to limbic areas. Proc Natl Acad Sci USA 100: 5497–5502.

Chomsky Noam, (2017) Requiem for the American Dream

Chomsky Noam, (2016) Who Rules the World?

Chomsky Noam, (2010) How the World Works

Churchland, P.S. (1986), Neurophilosophy (Cambridge, MA: The MIT Press).

Churchland, P.S. & Ramachandran, V.S. (1993), 'Filling in: Why Dennett is wrong', in Dennett and His Critics: Demystifying Mind, ed. B. Dahlbom (Oxford: Blackwell Scientific Press).

Churchland, P.S., Ramachandran, V.S. & Sejnowski, T.J. (1994), 'A critique of pure vision', in Large- scale Neuronal Theories of the Brain, ed. C. Koch & J.L. Davis (Cambridge, MA: The MIT Press).

Coyle EF. Integration of the physiological factors determining endurance performance ability. Exerc Sport Sci Rev. 1995;23:25–63.

Crick, F. (1994), The Astonishing Hypothesis: The Scientific Search for the Soul (New York: Simon and Schuster).

Crick, F. (1996), 'Visual perception: rivalry and consciousness', Nature, 379.

Crick, F. & Koch, C. (1992), 'The problem of consciousness', Scientific American, 267.

Damasio, A (2003a) Looking for Spinoza. Harcourt Inc. Damasio A (2003b) Feeling of emotion and the self. Ann NY Acad Sci 1001: 253–261.

d'Aquili, Eugene. "Senses of Reality in Science and Religion." Zygon 17, no 4 (1982)

d'Aquili, Eugene. "The Biopsychological Determinants of Religious Ritual Behavior." Zygon 10, no. 1 (1975)

d'Aquili, Eugene. "The Myth-Ritual Complex: A Biogenetic Structural Analysis." Zygon 18, no. 3 (1983)

d'Aquili, Eugene, and Andrew Newberg. The Mystical Mind: Probing the Biology of Religious Experience. Minneapolis: Fortress Press, 1999.

Daly DD. 1958. Ictal affect. Am J Psychiatry.

Damasio, A. (1994) Descartes' Error: Emotion, Reason and the Human Brain. New York, Putnams.

Damasio, A. (1999) The Feeling of What Happens: Body, Emotion and the Making of Consciousness. London, Heinemann.

Darwin, C. (1859) On the Origin of Species by Means of Natural Selection. London, Murray.

Darwin, C. (1871) The Descent of Man and Selection in Relation to Sex. London, John Murray.

Darwin, C. (1872) The Expression of the Emotions in Man and Animals. London, John Murray; also published 1965, Chicago, University of Chicago Press.

Dawkins, M.S. (1987) Minding and mattering. In C. Blakemore and S. Greenfield (eds) Mindwaves. Oxford, Blackwell, 151-60.

Dawkins, R. (1976) The Selfish Gene. Oxford, Oxford University Press; a new edition, with additional material, was published in 1989.

Di Pellegrino G, Fadiga L, Fogassi L, Gallese V, Rizzolatti G (1992) Understanding motor events: A neurophysiological study. Exp Brain Res 91: 176–80.

Deikman, A.J. (2000) A functional approach to mysticism. Journal of Consciousness Studies 7(11-12), 75-91.

Delmonte, M.M. (1987) Personality and meditation. In M. West (ed.) The Psychology of Meditation. Oxford, Clarendon Press, 118-32.

Dennett, D.C. (1988) Quining qualia. In A.J. Marcel and E. Bisiach (eds) Consciousness in Contemporary Science. Oxford, Oxford University Press, 42-77.

Dennett, D.C. (1991) Consciousness Explained. Boston, MA, and London, Little, Brown and Co.

Dennett, D.C. (1995a) Darwin's Dangerous Idea. London, Penguin.

Dennett, D.C. (1998b) Brainchildren: Essays on Designing Minds. Cambridge, MA, MIT Press.

Dewhurst, Kenneth, and A. W. Beard. "Sudden Religious Conversions in Temporal Lobe Epilepsy." British Journal of Psychiatry 117 (1970)

Dewhurst K, Beard AW. Sudden religious conversions in temporal lobe epilepsy. 1970 Epilepsy Behav 2003

Devinsky O, Lai G. Spirituality and religion in epilepsy. Epilepsy Behav 2008.

Devinsky, O., Morrell, MJ, Vogt, BA. (1995) 'Contribution of anterior cingulate cortex to behavior', Brain, 118.

E. Horvitz, "One Hundred Year Study on Artificial Intelligence: Reflections and Framing," ed: Stanford University, 2014.

Eckhart Meister, Selected Writings

Egidi R., ed. (1999), "Von Wright and 'Dante's Dream': Stages in a Philosophical Pilgrim's Progress", in

In Search of a New Humanism: the Philosophy of G.H. von Wright, ed. by R. Egidi, Kluwer, Dordrecht.

Fadiga L, Fogassi L, Pavesi G, Rizzolatti G (1995) Motor facilitation during action observation: a magnetic stimulation study. J Neurophysiol 73: 2608–2611.

Fogassi L, Gallese V, Fadiga L, Rizzolatti G (1998) Neurons responding to the sight of goal directed hand/arm actions in the parietal area PF (7b) of the macaque monkey. Soc Neurosci Abs 24:257.5.

Frith U, Frith CD (2003) Development and neurophysiology of mentalizing. Philos Trans R Soc Lond B Biol Sci 358: 459.

Farah, M.J. (1989), 'The neural basis of mental imagery', Trends in Neurosciences, 10.

Finlay BL, Darlington RB (1995) Linked regularities in the development and evolution of mammalian brains. Science 268.

Freud, S. "The Interpretation of Dreams", 1900

Freud, S. "Selected papers on hysteria and other psychoneuroses" Journal of Nervous and Mental Disease 1909.

Freud, S. "The Origin and Development of Psychoanalysis", 1910

Freud, S. "Psychopathology of everyday life", 1914

Freud, S. "Beyond the Pleasure Principle", 1920

Frith, C.D. & Dolan, R.J. (1997), 'Abnormal beliefs: Delusions and memory', Paper presented at the May, 1997, Harvard Conference on Memory and Belief.

Gay, Volney, ed. Neuroscience and Religion. Plymouth, UK: Lexington Books, 2009.

Gazzaniga, M. S. (1985). The social brain. New York: Basic Books.

Gazzaniga, M.S. (1993), 'Brain mechanisms and conscious experience', Ciba Foundation Symposium, 174.

Geschwind N. "Behavioural changes in temporal lobe epilepsy". Psychol Med. 1979.

Gellhorn, E., Kiely, W.F. "Mystical states of consciousness: neurophysiological and clinical aspects." J Nerv Ment Dis. 1972;154:399-405.

Gilbert SL, Dobyns WB, Lahn BT (2005) Genetic links between brain development and brain evolution. Nat Rev Genet 6.

Gray JA. The Psychology of Fear and Stress. 2nd ed. New York, NY: Cambridge University Press; 1988.

Gloor, P. (1992), 'Amygdala and temporal lobe epilepsy', in The Amygdala: Neurobiological Aspects of Emotion, Memory and Mental Dysfunction, ed J.P. Aggleton (New York: Wiley-Liss).

Greenspan, S. I. and S. G. Shanker (2004). The first idea: How symbols, language, and intelligence evolved from our early primate ancestors to modern humans. Cambridge, MA: Da Capo Press.

Grady, D. (1993), 'The vision thing: Mainly in the brain', Discover, June.

Gallagher HL, Frith CD (2003) Functional imaging of 'theory of mind'. Trends Cogn Sci 7: 77.

Gallese V, Fogassi L, Fadiga L, Rizzolatti G (2002) Action representation and the inferior parietal lobule. In: Prinz W, Hommel B (eds) Attention & Performance XIX. Common mechanisms in perception and action. Oxford University Press, Oxford.

Gallese V, Keysers C, Rizzolatti G (2004) A unifying view of the basis of social cognition. Trends Cogn Sci 8: 396–403.

Goldman AI, Sripada CS (2004) Simulationist models of face-based emotion recognition. Cognition 94: 193–213.

Grèzes J, Costes N, Decety J (1998) Top-down effect of strategy on the perception of human biological motion: a PET investigation. Cogn Neuropsychol 15: 553–582.

Grèzes J, Armony JL, Rowe J, Passingham RE (2003) Activations related to "mirror" and "canonical" neurones in the human brain: an fMRI study. Neuroimage 18: 928–937.

Gross CG, Rocha-Miranda CE, Bender DB (1972) Visual properties of neurons in the inferotemporal cortex of the macaque. J Neurophysiol 35: 96–111.

Guevara Che, The Motorcycle Diaries, 1992

Hari R, Forss N, Avikainen S, Kirveskari S, Salenius S, Rizzolatti G (1998) Activation of human primary motor cortex during action observation: a neuromagnetic study. Proc. Natl Acad Sci USA 95: 15061–15065.

Hardy, G. H. (1940). Ramanujan. Cambridge: Cambridge University Press.

Hall, Daniel, Keith Meador, and Harold Koenig. "Measuring Religiousness in Health Research: Review and Critique." Journal of Religion and Health 47, no. 2 (2008)

Harris, Sam, Jonas Kaplan, Ashley Curiel, Susan Bookheimer, Marco Iacoboni, and Mark Cohen. "The Neural Correlates of Religious and

Nonreligious Belief." PLoS One 4, no. 10 (October 1, 2009)

Halgren, E. (1992), 'Emotional neurophysiology of the amygdala within the context of human cognition', in The Amygdala: Neurobiological Aspects of Emotion, Memory and Mental Dysfunction, ed J.P. Aggleton (New York: Wiley-Liss).

Halligan PW, Fink GR, Marshal JC, Vallar G. 2003. Spatial cognition: evidence from visual neglect. Trends Cogn Sci.

Handbook of Emotions, Edited by Michael Lewis, Jeannette M. Haviland-Jones, and Lisa Feldman Barrett, The Guilford Press; 3rd edition (2010).

Hameroff, S.R. and Penrose, R. (1996) Conscious events as orchestrated space-time selections. Journal of Consciousness Studies 3(1), 36-53; also reprinted in J. Shear (ed.) (1997) Explaining Consciousness-The Hard

Problem. Cambridge, MA, MIT Press, 177-95.

Harding, D.E. (1961) On Having no Head: Zen and the Re-Discovery of the Obvious. London, Buddhist Society.

Hardy, A. (1979) The Spiritual Nature of Man: A Study of Contemporary Religious Experience. Oxford, Clarendon Press.

Harre, R. and Gillett, G. (1994) The Discursive Mind. Thousand Oaks, CA, Sage.

Haugeland, J. (ed.) (1997) Mind Design II: Philosophy, Psychology, Artificial Intelligence. Cambridge, MA, MIT Press.

Hauser, M.D. (2000) Wild Minds: What Animals Really Think. New York, Henry Holt and Co.; London, Penguin.

Hebb, D.O. (1949) The Organization of Behavior. New York, Wiley.

Helmholtz, H.L.F. von (1856-67) Treatise on Physiological Optics.

Hess, EH (1975) "The role of pupil size in communication," Scientific American, 233(5), 110–12.

Heyes, C.M. (1998) Theory of mind in nonhuman primates. Behavioral and Brain Sciences 21, 101-48; with commentaries.

Heyes, C.M. and Galef, B.G. (eds) (1996) Social Learning in Animals: The Roots of Culture. San Diego, CA, Academic Press.

Hilgard, E.R. (1986) Divided Consciousness: Multiple Controls in Human Thought and Action. New York, Wiley.

Hilton, E.N., Lundberg, T.R. Transgender Women in the Female Category of Sport: Perspectives on Testosterone Suppression and Performance Advantage. Sports Med 51, 199–214 (2021).

Hitler, Adolf. Mein Kampf, 1925

Hodgson, R. (1891) A case of double consciousness. Proceedings of the Society for Psychical Research 7, 221-58.

Hofstadter, D.R. and Dennett, D.C. (eds) (1981) The Mind's I: Fantasies and Reflections on Self and Soul. London, Penguin.

Holland, J. (ed.) (2001) Ecstasy: The Complete Guide: A Comprehensive Look at the Risks and Benefits of MDMA. Rochester, VT, Park Street Press.

Holmes, D.S. (1987) The influence of meditation versus rest on physiological arousal. In M. West (ed.) The Psychology of Meditation. Oxford, Clarendon Press, 81-103.

Holmstrom, David. 1992, Christian Science Monitor

Holt, J. (1999) Blindsight in debates about qualia. Journal of Consciousness Studies 6(5), 54-71.

Holloway RL (1996) Evolution of the human brain. In: Lock A, Peters CR (eds) Handbook of human symbolic evolution. Oxford University Press, Oxford

Iacoboni M, Woods RP, Brass M, Bekkering H, Mazziotta JC, Rizzolatti G (1999) Cortical mechanisms of human imitation. Science 286: 2526–2528.

Iacoboni M, Koski LM, Brass M, Bekkering H, Woods RP, Dubeau MC, Mazziotta JC, Rizzolatti G (2001) Reafferent copies of imitated actions in the right superior temporal cortex. Proc Natl Acad Sci USA 98: 13995–13999.

Jeannerod M (1988) The neural and behavioural organization of goal-directed movements. Clarendon Press, Oxford.

Johnson-Frey SH, Maloof FR, Newman-Norlund R, Farrer C, Inati S, Grafton ST (2003) Actions or hand-objects interactions? Human inferior frontal cortex and action observation. Neuron 39: 1053–1058.

Jackson, F. (1982) Epiphenomenal qualia. Philosophical Quarterly 32, 127-36.

James, W. (1890) The Principles of Psychology (2 volumes). London, Macmillan.

James, W. (1902) The Varieties of Religious Experience: A Study in Human Nature. New York and London, Longmans, Green and Co.

Jansen, K. (2001) Ketamine: Dreams and Realities. Sarasota, FL, Multidisciplinary Association for Psychedelic Studies.

Jay, M. (ed.) (1999) Artificial Paradises: A Drugs Reader. London, Penguin.

Jaynes, J. (1976) The Origin of Consciousness in the Breakdown of the Bicameral Mind. New York, Houghton Mifflin.

Johnson, M.K. and Raye, C.L. (1981) Reality monitoring. Psychological Review 88, 67-85.

Kadim I, Mahgoub O, Baqir S et al. (2015) Cultured meat from muscle stem cells: a review of challenges and prospects. J Integr Agr 14: 222–233

Kandel, E. R. In Search of Memory: The Emergence of a New Science of Mind, W. W. Norton & Company (2007).

Kandel E. R. Schwartz JH, Jessel TM. Principles of neural sciences. New York; McGraw Hill, 2000.

Kanwisher, N. (2001) Neural events and perceptual awareness. Cognition

79, 89-113; also reprinted inS. Dehaene (ed.) The Cognitive Neuroscience of Consciousness. Cambridge, MA, MIT Press, 89-113.

Karn, K. and Hayhoe, M. (2000) Memory representations guide targeting eye movements in a natural task. Visual Cognition 7, 673-703.

Kennedy, H., & Dehay, C. (1988). Functional implications of the anatomical organization of the callosal projections of visual areas V1 and V2 in the macaque monkey. Behav. Brain Res., 29, 225–236.

Kentridge, R.W. and Heywood, C.A. (1999) The status of blindsight. Journal of Consciousness Studies 6(5), 3-11.

Kihlstrom, J.F. (1996) Perception without awareness of what is perceived, learning without awareness of what is learned. In M. Velmans (ed.) The Science of Consciousness. London, Routledge, 23-46.

Kosslyn, S.M. (1980) Image and Mind. Cambridge, MA, Harvard University Press.

Kosslyn, S.M. (1988) Aspects of a cognitive neuroscience of mental imagery. Science 240, 1621-6.

Kinsbourne, M. (1995), 'The intralaminar thalamic nucleii', Consciousness and Cognition, 4.

Kjaer, Troels, Camilla Bertelsen, Paola Piccini, David Brooks, Jorgen Alving, and Hans Lou. "Increased Dopamine Tone during Meditation- Induced Change of Consciousness." Cognitive Brain Research 13, no. 2 (April 2002)

Kölmel HW. 1985. Complex visual hallucinations in the hemianopic field. J Neurol Neurosurg Psychiatry.

Koenig, Harold. "Research on Religion, Spirituality, and Mental Health: A Review." Canadian Journal of Psychiatry 54, no. 5 (May 2009)

Koenig, Harold, ed. Handbook of Religion and Mental Health. San Diego, CA: Academic Press, 1998

Kraepelin E. Psychiatry: A Textbook for Students and Physicians. New York, NY: Science History Publications; 1990.

Lauglin, Charles, John McManus, and Eugene d'Aquili. Brain, Symbol, and Experience. 2nd ed. New York: Columbia University Press, 1992

Lakoff, G. and M. Johnson (1999). Philosophy in the flesh. Basic Books: New York.

LeDoux, J. E. (1996). The emotional brain. New York: Simon & Schuster.

LeDoux, J.E. (1992), 'Emotion and the amygdala', in The Amygdala: Neurobiological Aspects of Emo- tion, Memory and Mental Dysfunction, ed J.P. Aggleton (New York: Wiley-Liss).

Levin, D.T. and Simons, D.J. (1997) Failure to detect changes to attended objects in motion pictures. Psychonomic Bulletin and Review 4, 501-6.

Levine,J. (1983) Materialism and qualia: the explanatory gap. Pacific Philosophical Quarterly 64, 354-61.

Levine,J. (2001) Purple Haze: The Puzzle of Consciousness. New York, Oxford University Press. Levine, S. (1979) A Gradual Awakening. New York, Doubleday.

Levinson, B.W. (1965) States of awareness during general anaesthesia. British Journal of Anaesthesia 37, 544-6.

Lewicki, P., Czyzewska, M. and Hoffman, H. (1987) Unconscious acquisition of complex procedural knowledge. Journal of Experimental Psychology: Learning, Memory and Cognition 13, 523-30.

Lewicki, P., Hill, T. and Bizot, E. (1988) Acquisition of procedural knowledge about a pattern of stimuli that cannot be articulated. Cognitive Psychology 20, 24-37.

Lewicki, P., Hill, T. and Czyzewska, M. (1992) Nonconscious acquisition of information. American Psychologist 47, 796-801.

Manthey S, Schubotz RI, von Cramon DY (2003). Premotor cortex in observing erroneous action: an fMRI study. Brain Res Cogn Brain Res 15: 296–307.

Mesulam MM, Mufson EJ (1982) Insula of the old world monkey. III: Efferent cortical output and comments on function. J Comp Neurol 212: 38–52.

Naskar, Abhijit. "Homo: A Brief History of Consciousness", 2015

Naskar, Abhijit. "What is Mind?", 2016

Naskar, Abhijit. "Love, God & Neurons: Memoir of A Scientist who found himself by getting lost", 2016

Naskar, Abhijit. "Principia Humanitas", 2017

Naskar, Abhijit. "We Are All Black: A Treatise on Racism", 2017

Naskar, Abhijit. "Either Civilized or Phobic: A Treatise on Homosexuality", 2017

Naskar, Abhijit. "The Bengal Tigress: A Treatise on Gender Equality", 2017

Naskar, Abhijit. "Morality Absolute", 2017

Naskar, Abhijit. "Build Bridges not Walls: In the name of Americana", 2018

Naskar, Abhijit. "Fabric of Humanity", 2018

Naskar, Abhijit. "Citizens of Peace: Beyond the Savagery of Sovereignty", 2019

Naskar, Abhijit. "The Constitution of The United Peoples of Earth", 2019

Naskar, Abhijit. "Neurons Giveth, Neurons Taketh Away | Abhijit Naskar | TEDxIIMRanchi", 2019 https://www.youtube.com/watch?v=B NX-Q0ySm80

Naskar, Abhijit. "Mission Reality", 2019

Naskar, Abhijit. "Operation Justice: To Make A Society That Needs No Law", 2019

Naskar, Abhijit. "Every Generation Needs Caretakers: The Gospel of Patriotism", 2020

Naskar, Abhijit. "Hurricane Humans: Give me accountability, I'll give you peace", 2020

Naskar, Abhijit. "Revolution Indomable", 2020

Naskar, Abhijit. "Servitude is Sanctitude", 2020

Naskar, Abhijit. "Good Scientist: When Science and Service Combine", 2020

Newberg, Andrew, and Jeremy Iversen. "The Neural Basis of the Complex Mental Task of Meditation: Neurotransmitter and Neurochemical Considerations." Medical Hypotheses 61, no. 2 (2003).

Newberg, Andrew. "How God Changes Your Brain: An Introduction to Jewish Neurotheology", CCAR Journal: The Reform Jewish Quarterly, Winter 2016.

Newberg, Andrew, and Stephanie Newberg. "A Neuropsychological Perspective on Spiritual Development." In Handbook of Spiritual Development in Childhood and Adolescence, edited by Eugene

Roehlkepartain, Pamela King, Linda Wagener, and Peter Benson. London: Sage Publications, Inc., 2005

Newberg, Andrew. "The Neurotheology Link An Intersection Between Spirituality and Health", Alternative and Complimentary Therapies, Vol 21 No 1, February 2015.

Newberg, Andrew, Nancy Wintering, Dharma Khalsa, Hannah Roggenkamp, and Mark Waldman. "Meditation Effects on Cognitive Function and Cerebral Blood Flow in Subjects with Memory Loss: A Preliminary Study." Journal of Alzheimer's Disease 20, no. 2 (2010)

Nash, M. (1995), 'Glimpses of the mind', Time.

Nesse RM. Proximate and evolutionary studies of anxiety, stress and depression: synergy at the interface. Neurosci Biobehav Rev. 1999;23:895-903.

Nicolelis, Miguel. (2011) "Beyond Boundaries: The New Neuroscience of Connecting Brains with Machines---and How It Will Change Our Lives", Times Books

O'Hara, K. and Scutt, T. (1996) There is no hard problem of consciousness. Journal of Consciousness Studies 3(4), 290-302, reprinted in J. Shear (ed.) (1997) Explaining Consciousness. Cambridge, MA, MIT Press, 69-82.

O'Regan, J.K. (1992) Solving the "real" mysteries of visual perception: the world as an outside memory. Canadian Journal of Psychology 46, 461-88.

O'Regan, J.K. and Noe, A. (2001) A sensorimotor account of vision and visual consciousness. Behavioral and Brain Sciences 24(5), 883-917.

O'Regan, J.K., Rensink, R.A. and Clark,].]. (1999) Change-blindness as a result of "mudsplashes." Nature 398, 34.

Ornstein, R.E. (1977) The Psychology of Consciousness (2nd edn). New York, Harcourt.

Ornstein, R.E. (1986) The Psychology of Consciousness (3rd edn). New York, Pehguin.

Ornstein, R.E. (1992) The Evolution of Consciousness. New York, Touchstone.

Penfield W, Faulk ME (1955) The insula: further observations on its function. Brain 78: 445– 470.

Penrose, R. (1994), Shadows of the Mind (Oxford: Oxford University Press).

Penrose, R. (1989), The Emperor's New Mind: Concerning Computers, Minds and The Laws of Physics (Oxford: Oxford University Press).

Persinger, "'I would kill in God's name' role of sex, weekly church attendance, report of a religious experience and limbic lability" Perceptual and Motor Skills 1997.

Persinger "Experimental simulation of the God experience" Neurotheology 2003.

Persinger, Corradini, Clement, Keaney, et al "Neurotheology and its convergence with neuroquantology" NeuroQuantology 2010.

Persinger, Koren and St-Pierre "The electromagnetic induction of mystical and altered states within the laboratory" Journal of Consciousness Exploration and Research 2010.

Persinger "Case report: A prototypical spontaneous 'sensed presence' of a sentient being and concomitant electroencephalographic activity in the clinical laboratory" Neurocase 2008.

Persinger and Saroka "Potential production of Hughlings Jackson's "parasitic consciousness" by physiologically-patterned weak transcerebral magnetic fields: QEEG and source localization" Epilepsy & Behavior 28 (2013).

Persinger. "The neuropsychiatry of paranormal experiences". J Neuropsychiatry Clin Neurosci 2001.

Persinger. "Neuropsychological bases of god beliefs", New York: Praeger, 1987

Persinger. "Temporal lobe epileptic signs and correlative behaviors displayed by normal populations", Journal of General Psychology, 1986

Perry BD, Pollard R. Homeostasis, stress, trauma, and adaptation. A neurodevelopmental view of childhood trauma. Child Adolesc Psychiatr Clin N Am. 1998;7:33.

Paré, D. & Llinás, R. (1995), 'Conscious and preconscious processes as seen from the standpoint of sleep-waking cycle neurophysiology', Neuropsychologia, 33.

Phillips ML, Young AW, Senior C, Brammer M, Andrew C, Calder AJ, Bullmore ET, Perrett DI, Rowland D, Williams SC, Gray JA, David AS (1997) A specific neural substrate for perceiving facial expressions of disgust. Nature 389: 495–498.

Phillips ML, Young AW, Scott SK, Calder AJ, Andrew C, Giampietro V, Williams SC, Bullmore ET, Brammer M, Gray JA (1998) Neural responses to facial and vocal expressions of fear and disgust. Proc R Soc Lond B Biol Sci 265: 1809–1817.

Puce A, Perrett D (2003) Electrophysiological and brain imaging of biological motion. Philosoph Trans Royal Soc Lond, Series B, 358: 435–445.

Ramachandran VS. Behavioral and magnetoencephalographic correlates of plasticity in the adult human brain. Proc Natl Acad Sci USA 1993; 90: 10413–20.

Ramachandran VS. Phantom limbs, neglect syndromes, repressed memories, and Freudian psychology. Int Rev Neurobiol 1994; 37: 291–333.

Ramachandran VS. Plasticity and functional recovery in neurology. Clin Med 2005; 5: 368–73.

Ramachandran VS, Hirstein W. The perception of phantom limbs. The D. O. Hebb lecture. Brain 1998; 121: 1603–30.

Ramachandran VS, Rogers-Ramachandran D, Cobb S. Touching the phantom limb. Nature 1995; 377: 489–90.

Ramachandran VS, Rogers-Ramachandran D. Phantom limbs and

neural plasticity. Arch Neurol 2000; 57: 317–20.

Ramachandran VS, Rogers-Ramachandran D. It's all done with mirrors. Sci Am Mind 2007; 18: 16–9.

Ramachandran VS, Rogers-Ramachandran D. Sensations referred to a patient's phantom arm from another subjects intact arm: perceptual correlates of mirror neurons. Med Hypotheses 2008; 70: 1233–4.

Ramachandran VS, Rogers-Ramachandran D, Stewart M. Perceptual correlates of massive cortical reorganization. Science 1992; 258: 1159–60.

Rizzolatti G, Craighero L (2004) The mirror-neuron system. Annu Rev Neurosci 27: 169–192.

Rizzolatti G, Fogassi L, Gallese V (2001) Neurophysiological mechanisms underlying the understanding and imitation of action. Nature Rev Neurosci 2:661–670.

Rock I, Victor J. Vision and touch: an experimentally created conflict between the two senses. Science 1964; 143: 594–6.

Rose´n B, Lundborg G. Training with a mirror in rehabilitation of the hand. Scand J Plast Reconstr Surg Hand Surg 2005; 39: 104–8.

Roberts, TA; Smalley, J; Ahrendt, D (December 2020). "Effect of gender affirming hormones on athletic performance in transwomen and transmen: implications for sporting organisations and legislators". British Journal of Sports Medicine. 55 (11): 577–583

Royet JP, Plailly J, Delon-Martin C, Kareken DA, Segebarth C (2003) fMRI of emotional responses to odors: influence of hedonic valence and judgment, handedness, and gender. Neuroimage 20: 713–728.

Rozin R Haidt J and McCauley CR (2000) Disgust. In: Lewis M, Haviland-Jones JM (eds) Handbook of Emotion. 2nd Edition. Guilford Press, New York, pp 637–653.

Saxe R, Carey S, Kanwisher N (2004) Understanding other minds: linking developmental psychology and functional neuroimaging. Annu Rev Psychol 55: 87–124.

S. J. Russell and P. Norvig, Artificial intelligence: a modern approach (3rd edition): Prentice Hall, 2009.

Singer T, Seymour B, O'Doherty J, Kaube H, Dolan RJ, Frith CD (2004) Empathy for pain involves the affective but not the sensory components of pain. Science 303: 1157–1162.

Smith A (1759) The theory of moral sentiments (ed. 1976). Clarendon Press, Oxford.

Schilling, Vincent. 2017, indian country today

Stein, Stephen K. 2017, The Sea in World History: Exploration, Travel, and Trade

Simonsen R (2015) Eating for the future: veganism and the challenge of in vitro meat. In: Stapleton P, Byers A (Hg). Biopolitics and utopia. Palgrave Macmillan, New York (2015), S 167–190

Tesla N. "My Inventions", 1919

T. R. Society, "Machine learning: the power and promise of computers that learn by example," ed. The Royal Society, 2017.

Tomasello M, Call J (1997) Primate cognition. Oxford University Press, Oxford.

www.ingramcontent.com/pod-product-compliance
Lightning Source LLC
Chambersburg PA
CBHW051256250726
48656CB00004B/1324